Your 5-Week Work Year

80/20 Productivity Planner

"Some people dream of success while other people wake up every morning and make it happen"

Your 5-Week Work Year Begins NOW

The Focusing Question

**"What's the ONE Thing I can do
[goal] [time frame] such that by doing it
everything else will be easier or unnecessary?"**

For Example:

- For my job, what's the ONE Thing I can do to ensure I hit my goals today such that by doing it everything else will be easier or unnecessary?"
- For my health, what's the ONE Thing I can do to achieve my diet goals this week such that by doing it everything else will be easier or unnecessary?
- For my key relationships, what's the ONE Thing I can do to improve my relationship with my spouse/partner this month such that by doing it everything else will be easier or unnecessary?
- For my business, what's the ONE Thing I can do to make us more competitive this quarter such that by doing it everything else will be easier or unnecessary?
- For my finances, what's the ONE Thing I can do to increase my net worth this year such that by doing it everything else will be easier or unnecessary?

- (from https://www.samuelthomasdavies.com/the-focusing-question/)

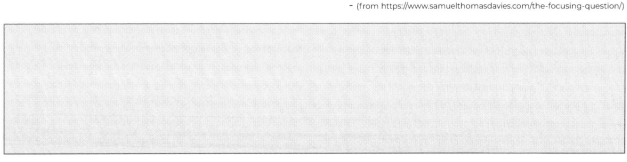

Then Identify and Focus on the Daily Tasks that Cause this Result

My Monthly PLANNER

MONTH:

TOP PRIORITY

TOP GOALS

Monday	Tuesday	Wednesday	Thursday	Friday	Saturday	Sunday

NOTES:

WEEKLY planner

WEEK OF:

TOP WEEKLY GOALS

HOW I'M GOING TO ACCOMPLISH MY GOALS

	URGENT	NOT URGENT
IMPORTANT		
NOT IMPORTANT		

DAILY priority

DATE

M T W T F S S

MY TOP OUTCOMES OF THE DAY

01
02
03

Today's To-Do List

HOUR-by-hour SCHEDULE

06
07
08
09
10
11
12
01
02
03
04
05
06
07
08
09
10

NOTES

REMINDERS

ACCOMPLISHMENTS

my deep work hours log

TASK DETAILS | date | hours

TOTAL HOURS

DAILY priority

DATE

M T W T F S S

MY TOP OUTCOMES OF THE DAY

01
02
03

Today's To-Do List

HOUR-by-hour SCHEDULE

06
07
08
09
10
11
12
01
02
03
04
05
06
07
08
09
10

NOTES	REMINDERS	ACCOMPLISHMENTS

my deep work hours log

TASK DETAILS | date | hours

TOTAL HOURS

DAILY priority

DATE

M T W T F S S

MY TOP OUTCOMES OF THE DAY

01
02
03

Today's To-Do List

HOUR-by-hour SCHEDULE

06
07
08
09
10
11
12
01
02
03
04
05
06
07
08
09
10

NOTES

REMINDERS

ACCOMPLISHMENTS

my deep work hours log

TASK DETAILS | date | hours

TOTAL HOURS

DAILY priority

DATE

M T W T F S S

MY TOP OUTCOMES OF THE DAY

01
02
03

Today's To-Do List

HOUR-by-hour SCHEDULE

06
07
08
09
10
11
12
01
02
03
04
05
06
07
08
09
10

NOTES

REMINDERS

ACCOMPLISHMENTS

my deep work hours log

TASK DETAILS	date	hours

TOTAL HOURS

DAILY priority

DATE

M T W T F S S

MY TOP OUTCOMES OF THE DAY

01 ....
02 ....
03 ....

Today's To-Do List

HOUR-by-hour SCHEDULE

06
07
08
09
10
11
12
01
02
03
04
05
06
07
08
09
10

NOTES

REMINDERS

ACCOMPLISHMENTS

my deep work hours log

TASK DETAILS | date | hours

TOTAL HOURS

DAILY priority

DATE

M T W T F S S

MY TOP OUTCOMES OF THE DAY

01 ....
02 ....
03 ....

Today's To-Do List

HOUR-by-hour SCHEDULE

06
07
08
09
10
11
12
01
02
03
04
05
06
07
08
09
10

NOTES	REMINDERS	ACCOMPLISHMENTS

my deep work hours log

TASK DETAILS | date | hours

TOTAL HOURS

DAILY priority

DATE

M T W T F S S

MY TOP OUTCOMES OF THE DAY

01 ....
02 ....
03 ....

Today's To-Do List

HOUR-by-hour SCHEDULE

06
07
08
09
10
11
12
01
02
03
04
05
06
07
08
09
10

NOTES	REMINDERS	ACCOMPLISHMENTS

my deep work hours log

TASK DETAILS | date | hours

TOTAL HOURS

WEEKLY planner

WEEK OF:

TOP WEEKLY GOALS

HOW I'M GOING TO ACCOMPLISH MY GOALS

URGENT	NOT URGENT
IMPORTANT	
NOT IMPORTANT	

DAILY priority

DATE

M T W T F S S

MY TOP OUTCOMES OF THE DAY

01
02
03

Today's To-Do List

HOUR-by-hour SCHEDULE

06
07
08
09
10
11
12
01
02
03
04
05
06
07
08
09
10

NOTES

REMINDERS

ACCOMPLISHMENTS

my deep work hours log

TASK DETAILS — date — hours

TOTAL HOURS

DAILY priority

DATE

M T W T F S S

MY TOP OUTCOMES OF THE DAY

01
02
03

Today's To-Do List

HOUR-by-hour SCHEDULE

06
07
08
09
10
11
12
01
02
03
04
05
06
07
08
09
10

NOTES

REMINDERS

ACCOMPLISHMENTS

my deep work hours log

TASK DETAILS — date — hours

TOTAL HOURS

DAILY priority

DATE

M T W T F S S

MY TOP OUTCOMES OF THE DAY

01
02
03

Today's To-Do List

HOUR-by-hour SCHEDULE

06
07
08
09
10
11
12
01
02
03
04
05
06
07
08
09
10

NOTES

REMINDERS

ACCOMPLISHMENTS

my deep work hours log

TASK DETAILS   date   hours

TOTAL HOURS

DAILY priority

DATE

M T W T F S S

MY TOP OUTCOMES OF THE DAY

01
02
03

Today's To-Do List

HOUR-by-hour SCHEDULE

06
07
08
09
10
11
12
01
02
03
04
05
06
07
08
09
10

NOTES

REMINDERS

ACCOMPLISHMENTS

my deep work hours log

TASK DETAILS   date   hours

TOTAL HOURS

DAILY priority

DATE

M T W T F S S

MY TOP OUTCOMES OF THE DAY

01 ....
02 ....
03 ....

Today's To-Do List

HOUR-by-hour SCHEDULE

06
07
08
09
10
11
12
01
02
03
04
05
06
07
08
09
10

NOTES	REMINDERS	ACCOMPLISHMENTS

my deep work hours log

TASK DETAILS | date | hours

TOTAL HOURS

DAILY priority

DATE

M T W T F S S

MY TOP OUTCOMES OF THE DAY

01
02
03

Today's To-Do List

HOUR-by-hour SCHEDULE

06
07
08
09
10
11
12
01
02
03
04
05
06
07
08
09
10

NOTES

REMINDERS

ACCOMPLISHMENTS

my deep work hours log

TASK DETAILS   date   hours

TOTAL HOURS

DAILY priority

DATE

M T W T F S S

MY TOP OUTCOMES OF THE DAY

01
02
03

Today's To-Do List

HOUR-by-hour SCHEDULE

06
07
08
09
10
11
12
01
02
03
04
05
06
07
08
09
10

NOTES

REMINDERS

ACCOMPLISHMENTS

… my deep work hours log

ASK DETAILS | date | hours

TOTAL HOURS

WEEKLY planner

WEEK OF:

TOP WEEKLY GOALS

HOW I'M GOING TO ACCOMPLISH MY GOALS

URGENT	NOT URGENT

DAILY priority

DATE

M T W T F S S

MY TOP OUTCOMES OF THE DAY

01
02
03

Today's To-Do List

HOUR-by-hour SCHEDULE

06
07
08
09
10
11
12
01
02
03
04
05
06
07
08
09
10

NOTES

REMINDERS

ACCOMPLISHMENTS

my deep work hours log

TASK DETAILS | date | hours

TOTAL HOURS

DAILY priority

DATE

M T W T F S S

MY TOP OUTCOMES OF THE DAY

01
02
03

Today's To-Do List

HOUR-by-hour SCHEDULE

06
07
08
09
10
11
12
01
02
03
04
05
06
07
08
09
10

NOTES

REMINDERS

ACCOMPLISHMENTS

my deep work hours log

TASK DETAILS   date   hours

TOTAL HOURS

DAILY priority

DATE

M T W T F S S

MY TOP OUTCOMES OF THE DAY

01
02
03

Today's To-Do List

HOUR-by-hour SCHEDULE

06
07
08
09
10
11
12
01
02
03
04
05
06
07
08
09
10

NOTES	REMINDERS	ACCOMPLISHMENTS

my deep work hours log

TASK DETAILS | date | hours

TOTAL HOURS

DAILY priority

DATE

M T W T F S S

MY TOP OUTCOMES OF THE DAY

01
02
03

Today's To-Do List

HOUR-by-hour SCHEDULE

06
07
08
09
10
11
12
01
02
03
04
05
06
07
08
09
10

NOTES

REMINDERS

ACCOMPLISHMENTS

my deep work hours log

TASK DETAILS | date | hours

TOTAL HOURS

DAILY priority

DATE

M T W T F S S

MY TOP OUTCOMES OF THE DAY

01
02
03

Today's To-Do List

HOUR-by-hour SCHEDULE

06
07
08
09
10
11
12
01
02
03
04
05
06
07
08
09
10

NOTES

REMINDERS

ACCOMPLISHMENTS

my deep work hours log

TASK DETAILS | date | hours

TOTAL HOURS

DAILY priority

DATE

M T W T F S S

MY TOP OUTCOMES OF THE DAY

01
02
03

Today's To-Do List

HOUR-by-hour SCHEDULE

06
07
08
09
10
11
12
01
02
03
04
05
06
07
08
09
10

NOTES

REMINDERS

ACCOMPLISHMENTS

my deep work hours log

TASK DETAILS | date | hours

TOTAL HOURS

DAILY priority

DATE

M T W T F S S

MY TOP OUTCOMES OF THE DAY

01
02
03

Today's To-Do List

HOUR-by-hour SCHEDULE

06
07
08
09
10
11
12
01
02
03
04
05
06
07
08
09
10

NOTES

REMINDERS

ACCOMPLISHMENTS

my deep work hours log

TASK DETAILS   date   hours

TOTAL HOURS

WEEKLY planner

WEEK OF:

TOP WEEKLY GOALS

HOW I'M GOING TO ACCOMPLISH MY GOALS

URGENT

NOT URGENT

DAILY priority

DATE

M T W T F S S

MY TOP OUTCOMES OF THE DAY

01
02
03

Today's To-Do List

HOUR-by-hour SCHEDULE

06
07
08
09
10
11
12
01
02
03
04
05
06
07
08
09
10

NOTES

REMINDERS

ACCOMPLISHMENTS

my deep work hours log

TASK DETAILS   date   hours

TOTAL HOURS

DAILY priority

DATE

M T W T F S S

MY TOP OUTCOMES OF THE DAY

01 ....
02 ....
03 ....

Today's To-Do List

HOUR-by-hour SCHEDULE

06
07
08
09
10
11
12
01
02
03
04
05
06
07
08
09
10

NOTES

REMINDERS

ACCOMPLISHMENTS

my deep work hours log

TASK DETAILS | date | hours

TOTAL HOURS

DAILY priority

DATE

M T W T F S S

MY TOP OUTCOMES OF THE DAY

01 ....
02 ....
03 ....

Today's To-Do List

HOUR-by-hour SCHEDULE

06
07
08
09
10
11
12
01
02
03
04
05
06
07
08
09
10

NOTES

REMINDERS

ACCOMPLISHMENTS

my deep work hours log

TASK DETAILS   date   hours

TOTAL HOURS

DAILY priority

DATE

M T W T F S S

MY TOP OUTCOMES OF THE DAY

01
02
03

Today's To-Do List

HOUR-by-hour SCHEDULE

06
07
08
09
10
11
12
01
02
03
04
05
06
07
08
09
10

NOTES

REMINDERS

ACCOMPLISHMENTS

my deep work hours log

TASK DETAILS | date | hours

TOTAL HOURS

DAILY priority

DATE

M T W T F S S

MY TOP OUTCOMES OF THE DAY

01
02
03

Today's To-Do List

HOUR-by-hour SCHEDULE

06
07
08
09
10
11
12
01
02
03
04
05
06
07
08
09
10

NOTES

REMINDERS

ACCOMPLISHMENTS

my deep work hours log

ASK DETAILS | date | hours

TOTAL HOURS

DAILY priority

DATE

M T W T F S S

MY TOP OUTCOMES OF THE DAY

01 ....

02 ....

03 ....

Today's To-Do List

HOUR-by-hour SCHEDULE

06
07
08
09
10
11
12
01
02
03
04
05
06
07
08
09
10

NOTES

REMINDERS

ACCOMPLISHMENTS

my deep work hours log

TASK DETAILS | date | hours

TOTAL HOURS

DAILY priority

DATE

M T W T F S S

MY TOP OUTCOMES OF THE DAY

01
02
03

Today's To-Do List

HOUR-by-hour SCHEDULE

06
07
08
09
10
11
12
01
02
03
04
05
06
07
08
09
10

NOTES

REMINDERS

ACCOMPLISHMENTS

my deep work hours log

TASK DETAILS | date | hours

TOTAL HOURS

WEEKLY planner

WEEK OF:

TOP WEEKLY GOALS

HOW I'M GOING TO ACCOMPLISH MY GOALS

URGENT	NOT URGENT

DAILY priority

DATE

M T W T F S S

MY TOP OUTCOMES OF THE DAY

01
02
03

Today's To-Do List

HOUR-by-hour SCHEDULE

06
07
08
09
10
11
12
01
02
03
04
05
06
07
08
09
10

NOTES   **REMINDERS**   **ACCOMPLISHMENTS**

my deep work hours log

TASK DETAILS | date | hours

TOTAL HOURS

DATE

M T W T F S S

MY TOP OUTCOMES OF THE DAY

01
02
03

Today's To-Do List

HOUR-by-hour SCHEDULE

06
07
08
09
10
11
12
01
02
03
04
05
06
07
08
09
10

NOTES

REMINDERS

ACCOMPLISHMENTS

my deep work hours log

TASK DETAILS | date | hours

TOTAL HOURS

DAILY priority

DATE

M T W T F S S

MY TOP OUTCOMES OF THE DAY

01
02
03

Today's To-Do List

HOUR-by-hour SCHEDULE

06
07
08
09
10
11
12
01
02
03
04
05
06
07
08
09
10

NOTES	REMINDERS	ACCOMPLISHMENTS

my deep work hours log

TASK DETAILS   date   hours

TOTAL HOURS

DAILY priority

DATE

M T W T F S S

MY TOP OUTCOMES OF THE DAY

01
02
03

Today's To-Do List

HOUR-by-hour SCHEDULE

06
07
08
09
10
11
12
01
02
03
04
05
06
07
08
09
10

NOTES | **REMINDERS** | **ACCOMPLISHMENTS**

my deep work hours log

TASK DETAILS | date | hours

TOTAL HOURS

DAILY priority

DATE

M T W T F S S

MY TOP OUTCOMES OF THE DAY

01
02
03

Today's To-Do List

HOUR-by-hour SCHEDULE

06
07
08
09
10
11
12
01
02
03
04
05
06
07
08
09
10

NOTES

REMINDERS

ACCOMPLISHMENTS

my deep work hours log

TASK DETAILS — date — hours

TOTAL HOURS

DAILY priority

DATE

M T W T F S S

MY TOP OUTCOMES OF THE DAY

01 ....
02 ....
03 ....

Today's To-Do List

HOUR-by-hour SCHEDULE

06
07
08
09
10
11
12
01
02
03
04
05
06
07
08
09
10

NOTES

REMINDERS

ACCOMPLISHMENTS

my deep work hours log

ASK DETAILS | date | hours

TOTAL HOURS

DAILY priority

DATE

M T W T F S S

MY TOP OUTCOMES OF THE DAY

01
02
03

Today's To-Do List

HOUR-by-hour SCHEDULE

06
07
08
09
10
11
12
01
02
03
04
05
06
07
08
09
10

NOTES

REMINDERS

ACCOMPLISHMENTS

my deep work hours log

TASK DETAILS | date | hours

TOTAL HOURS

Made in the USA
Columbia, SC
16 June 2021